THE EXPERT IN YOU

FIND YOUR VOICE, BUILD YOUR LEGACY

By Entrepreneur Encyclopedia

Visit

www.Entrepedia.co/FreeBooks
to receive Entrepedia books for FREE

www.Entrepedia.co/QuickStart
for your Entrepreneur Quick Start Guide

ABOUT ENTREPRENEUR ENCYCLOPEDIA

Our aim is to provide you with the knowledge you'll need to start a business from $0 and grow it to $100k per month in passive income.

You'll learn how to pick your niche, build a brand, drive free and paid traffic, deliver massive value, market your work, hire and outsource, systematize your process, scale and more.

Your destiny is up to you. Money can help you grow quickly but you don't need it. No banker or VC can tell you your idea is not good enough.

What you'll need to do is test the theories you develop, fail quickly and find products customers will pay you to create before spending a dime. Each step of the way you will be building an audience that will snowball into your inevitable success.

Being an entrepreneur requires you to learn an enormous amount of information on an endless variety of topics. You must find what's working, put your own spin on it, create massive value and give it to as many people as possible.

Today it's easier than ever to start a lifestyle business or grow a billion dollar company. But like anything, it requires effort, determination and a strong desire to help the world move in a positive direction.

Entrepreneur Encyclopedia is the shortest route to your dreams. Our books are designed to help you understand everything you need to know about each topic in under an hour.

Each one of our books will help you move your business forward in a vital area. Think of us like a mentor helping you break through plateaus and discover leading edge paths by showing you how to properly leverage today's best technology to be successful.

GIVING BACK

Entrepreneur Encyclopedia has taken the copyright off everything we publish and donate our material directly to the public domain. Powerful information like this should be available to anyone so they can benefit without restriction. Wisdom is for sharing. You can read the details on our uncopyright disclaimer.

EE is also teaming up with Kiva.org to help fund new projects by entrepreneurs in developing countries. Our aim is to provide 5% of our net sales to funding micro loans for people with a vision but without the ability to get loans from VCs or the banking system.

To minimize our footprint and help restore forests around the globe we are planting a tree for every 10 hardcover books we sell. You can read more about our mission at the back of this book. We pledge to put our clients and our world ahead of our profits.

Thanks for choosing Entrepreneur Encyclopedia and helping us help the planet.

Sincerely,

Travis & The Entrepedia Team

Uncopyright 2017 by Smart Reads, Inc. No rights reserved worldwide. Any part of this publication may be reproduced or transmitted in any form without the prior written consent of the publisher.

Disclaimer: The publisher and author make no representations or warranties with respect to the accuracy or completeness of these contents and disclaim all warranties for a particular purpose. The author or publisher is not responsible for how you use this information.

TABLE OF CONTENTS

Introduction	2
Understanding Expert Businesses	5
PART I: HOW TO BUILD A MASS MOVEMENT	8
Developing Your Charisma	9
Developing A Cause	22
A Fresh Start	28
Switching Opportunities	35
PART II: CREATING BELIEF	42
The One Big Thing	43
Bridging the Emotional Divide	45
Structuring Your Story	50
Scripting Your Epiphany Bridge Stories	55
False Mindsets	61
Three Belief Roadblocks	64
PART III: YOUR CALL OF DUTY	68
The Premium Offer	69
The Perfect Presentation	73
Putting Your Script Together	76
How To Break and Rebuild Belief Patterns	82
The Secret Weapon	88
Closing The Presentation	98

PART IV: THE FUNNELS	104
The Perfect Model For Webinar and Funnel	105
Closing in Four Questions	109
Perfect Webinar Cheat Sheet	113
Email Sequence Funnel	116
PART V: WHAT NOW?	118
Filling Your Funnel	119
Conclusion	123
Resources	125
Mission	128

INTRODUCTION

Every single one of us has an inborn gift. It could be knowledge you have; a rare ability, or a unique skill that you can impart to others. Whatever this gift is, it has the power to change your world and make you a wealthy person. The only thing you have to do is know how to apply it the right way.

In today's world, no commodity is more precious than information. People are willing to pay a lot of money to those who have access to special information and are willing to exchange it. However, this information must be relevant, applied with great skill, and exchanged at the right time.

In this book, *The Expert in You*, we lay down some of the most critical steps you can use to attract demand from the market and draw people who are ready to pay you for the information you have. You don't even need to have a business set up. Using the secrets revealed in this book, you can expect to create a profitable business from scratch. This book is not just a bunch of theoretical concepts. These are tried and tested techniques that, if applied correctly, can have you moving up the ladder from mere employee to business owner.

Yes, this book is for everyone who desires to succeed no matter where you may be right now. This may sound too much to believe, but let me remind you that you have something inside you that the world needs. All you have to do is be confident in presenting it to the world.

So what makes this book different from all the other business success books out there? Great question!

There are many books that can teach you how to make a lot of money, but we are more interested in helping you learn how to change lives! We want to help you grow so that you too can go out there and create a successful business that positively impacts the lives of other people. The money will always be there to be made, but the opportunity to touch lives in a positive way? That is what we are all about.

We strongly believe that you are already an expert at something. You may not have achieved the level of success you desire, but that's because nobody has shown you, step-by-step, how to take what you have and turn it into a customer magnet. This book breaks down the process of attaining business success in a way that makes it look simple. No matter what profession you are currently in – doctor, lawyer, shopkeeper, or self-employed - the contents of this book can help you grow your business.

If you have been mystified about how to make a lot of money using the knowledge you have, rest assured that you are now in possession of a book that will unravel that mystery. There is a path that leads to wealth and prosperity, and *The Expert in You* is where you begin the journey. Are you ready to learn and commit to taking action?

Let's begin!

UNDERSTANDING EXPERT BUSINESSES

One of the first lessons we need to talk about is the two types of expert business. Though they share similar tactics, there are differences that can help you understand which one to go for. They include:

1. **Selling Informational Material**

This is probably the one you will choose to create. It involves taking whatever unique life lessons you have learned and teaching it to others. This may be in the form of coaching, consulting, or creating informational products. This is one of the easiest ways to launch a startup because you can begin with no capital. All you need is a passion for teaching your content and exciting people using your stories.

Let's say you love playing basketball but your dunking skills aren't great. So you start researching ways of improving your vertical jump. You read every article and watch every video, and then you go out and practice every single idea. You then start recording videos of the different techniques you are using and post them on YouTube.

Initially, nobody cares much for your videos, but you keep going because you love it and just want to learn how to dunk. However, as time passes, you notice that your followers are increasing by the tens, then hundreds, and now you have thousands of people who are interested in learning how to dunk. You have now become an expert at something you love, and all you have to do is create and sell products that help people how to dunk.

The bottom line here is clear – The best way to grow your business is by sharing your knowledge and contributing to the success of others.

2. Growing a Company Using Informational Material

The second type of expert business involves using informational products to grow a company that already exists. It doesn't matter what kind of product or service your company provides: you can still sell informational products and acquire free customers in the process.

You can still succeed with this type of business even if you don't have startup capital. You can begin by becoming an expert, selling your information, and then using your existing customers to create a business. The customers are already primed for whatever you will be selling so you won't have to go out looking for them. Your information products will convince potential customers you are indeed an expert, and they will be willing to cough up more cash than they would elsewhere. On top of that, there will be no expenses whatsoever for drawing them in because they already paid you when they bought your information product! Ultimately, you will be able to grow your business at a much faster rate.

PART I: HOW TO BUILD A MASS MOVEMENT

If you are interested in sharing and converting your message into money, there is one thing you must learn to do. You must learn how to build an audience that resonates with your message. There's no point joining the long list of experts who are all talk but have no money to show for it, simply because no one is interested in what they have to say.

In this part of the book, we are going to examine how to get people to fall in love with your message and become your loyal supporters. You shall learn how to develop a charismatic character and get people to focus on a cause larger than themselves. Then you will learn how to offer your audience an opportunity they cannot afford to pass up.

Let's go and change some lives!

DEVELOPING YOUR CHARISMA

For a mass movement to be effective, it must be led by a charismatic leader. You may probably have looked in the mirror one time and wondered whether you are truly cut out for leadership. Maybe you don't even see yourself as an expert. One thing to remember is that you are not alone.

The truth is that a person grows into a leader when they start trying to become a master at something. Once they have learned as much as possible, they then begin to share this information with others so they too can grow. Most of the people who are amazing leaders also tend to doubt their own leadership qualities at some point, so just know you are in good company.

Leaders always feel a sense of wanting to help others improve their lives. Surprisingly enough, this internal desire is countered by another voice that constantly tells them they are not good enough. You would think this negative voice would dissipate over time, but it actually gets louder the more achievements you have. The point here is that even the most charismatic leaders suffer from self-doubt now and then, and that means you can become a leader, too.

There are many experts who do what they do simply because they want to make a difference in people's lives. They hear that negative voice and they choose to fight on. Unfortunately, there are many people who would have been experts right now but have chosen to listen to that inner critic. Instead of stepping up into leadership, they have ended up missing the opportunity to serve others with the talents that God blessed them with.

No matter what doubts you may have with your leadership abilities, all you need to know is that you have a responsibility to offer your gifts to the world around you. Those ideas, talents, and dreams that you hold are necessary to helping someone out there unlock their own gifts. Life is a long chain of people who have been positioned specifically to impact each other's destinies.

Can I tell you where the problem really lies? The reason you don't see yourself as uniquely gifted is because you have become accustomed to your own talents. You dismiss them as normal because they are second nature to you. But just because they've become "normal" for you, they're not normal for everybody else. They do not see your gift the same way you do. They look at you and wonder how you do what you do so easily. There are people out there waiting to pay

you a lot of money to make use of that one skill you are ignoring.
What does this mean? It means your gift is probably something that isn't a big deal to you. Maybe you were not born with it but have spent years studying, learning, and testing it. It could be something as simple as cooking, but to a person who can't cook, it's worth paying for. So the question you need to ask yourself right now is, "What is it that I find easy to do and absolutely love doing?"

It doesn't matter whether you have a degree or certificate in it. Most people worry too much about having the right papers before going out and doing anything in their lives. This is a common excuse, but the truth is that it is a pathetic one. All you need to know is how to get the right results. Period! If you are passionate about what you do, your results will be your certification.

It also doesn't matter whether other people are more knowledgeable than you in that particular field. Your job is to know more about the topic than the people whom you are teaching. There is always someone better than you at something, so instead of disregarding your skills as useless, learn from other experts and keep helping those who aren't as knowledgeable as you.

Identifying Your True Believers
Your true believers are the people who you want to serve with your expertise. So how exactly do you know who these people are? Well, ideally they should be those people who are in the same shoes you were in before you became an expert. Every charismatic leader leads people along a road they have been on themselves.

Identifying these people is often difficult, but there is a way to do it. There are generally three core markets every expert business depends on:

- Wealth
- Health
- Relationships

The question then becomes, "Which of these three markets match your field of expertise at this moment?"

Once you figure out which market you belong in, you will have to dig deeper to determine your target audience. But how do you do this?

Under each core market, there are several sub-markets. For example, the health market can be divided into nutrition, diet, weight loss, and the like. The wealth market can be divided into real estate, finance, sales, and investing. Relationships can be broken down into dating advice, parenting, marriage, etc. Of course, there can be many more sub-markets opening up at any given time.

The second question you need to answer is which submarket is aligned with your expertise at this moment? Maybe you have already figured this out already, but slow your horses a little bit. You won't make money from the submarkets. You have to dig a bit deeper until you get to the niches.

Take a good look at the other experts within the sub-market you fit into. What are they selling and what position can you occupy in that environment? What is going to make you stand out? Once you find something unique you can offer, that's your niche, and that is where you will make your wealth.

One of the problems most aspiring entrepreneurs have is that they want to dive into a niche that already exists, not realizing those are shark-infested waters. There are many other people who have already set up businesses within that niche and competition will be stiff. What you need to do is find a fresh niche for yourself that will open new opportunities. Rather than joining a niche that is already overloaded with competitors, be the first to create something new that others will want to join later on.

In case you are still unclear as to how to break down a core market into its niche, here are a few examples to help you out:

Core market - Health
Submarket – Nutrition
Niche – Low-fat diets

Core market – Wealth
Submarket – Online marketing
Niche – Selling e-commerce products on Twitter

Core market – Relationships
Submarket – Dating
Niche – Dating tips for introverts

Is Your Preferred Market Sustainable?
There are a number of things that you need to consider once you have found the right market for your business. What we recommend is you first back out of your preferred niche and look at the submarket. Remember that your sub-market is where your pool of

customers is, so the following considerations relate to your sub-market:

1. **Will the fresh niche you are creating excite customers in the submarket?** You need to be sure that whatever new opportunity you are presenting to them will get them excited.

2. **Is the sub-market passionate?** First of all, the first person that needs to be exuding passion about your particular niche is YOU. Do you find yourself constantly talking about your idea, even to the annoyance of your friends and family? If your answer is "Yes," then you are on the right track. So how do you know whether the submarket is also as passionate? Visit online communities and forums on social media and look at what people are engorging on. Try to find out whether your market has developed its own unique language because every passionate market does. Check out whether that market tends to hold seminars, conferences, or training summits, whether online or offline. If these events aren't happening, then you may find it difficult to draw people to your webinars and masterminds.

3. **Does the target audience have the willingness and ability to pay for information?** There are some customers who may want to pay but just don't have the money. Then there are those who do have the money but simply aren't willing to pay for information. You need a market that is both able and willing to pay for what you are offering.

EMBODYING THE CHARACTER OF A LEADER
What kind of character do you need to show to your audience to become the leader that they crave? The truth is that people are always looking for someone to step up and show them the way. Here are some key rules that can help you become the charismatic person to lead your movement:

Rule 1: Develop a character and life that your audience will be attracted to.
Why do you think your audience will want to follow you? The reason is simple: They see you in a position that they wish they could be in. They are attracted to you because you have walked the journey that they are still on, and they desire to attain the same outcome you have achieved. They want to bridge the gap between where they are and where you are standing, so they need you to teach them what to do. This is why you need to tell them your story about where you

came from and how you overcame hurdles. Showing your vulnerable side may be scary, but it will inspire others to want to change their lives.

Rule 2: Always be certain.
Let's be clear here, there is a huge difference between certainty and self-confidence. Self-confidence is just you being assured of your ability, while certainty is what gives you the ability to stand out as an expert and attract followers. It can take quite a while for you to develop certainty, but that is why it is important to share your message as often as possible so that you embody your own teachings. It doesn't matter whether people are following your blog, YouTube channel, or Twitter feed. Just keep at it every day until you find your own voice. This is more important in the initial stages than trying to get people to follow you. Soon enough, you will become what you teach, and people will see you as an expert.

Rule 3: Do not bore people.
You need to keep your audience fascinated about your teachings. Otherwise, you will not be able to form strong connections with your followers. Most of the experts who have great staying power tend to be highly prolific, but not in the way you think. Yes, being prolific means generating a high amount of content, but in this case, we are talking about coming up with

creative ideas that generate a big impact on people and earn you a lot of money.

Have you ever heard of the Prolific Index? This is a scale that describes the type of message you are sharing with your audience. At the center of the index, we have the mainstream ideas that everyone is sharing via traditional media. This is the stuff people can get for free online. It's boring, logical, and nobody is willing to pay money to learn it.

However, on the extremes of the index – on the far left and right - is what we refer to as "crazy zones." In this area, we have a few experts who have managed to convince some people to follow their ideas. The problem is that these ideas are so crazy that you cannot generate much wealth from them.

So where can you make your money then? In the area between the crazy and the mainstream zone! This is what we call the Prolific Zone. In this area, your message is unique enough for people to notice as well as fascinating enough for people to pay for it. This is where you need to be – creating a polarizing message that people are willing to try out.

There is one thing that we must warn you about. The more polarizing your message gets, the more hate you attract from the other side of the spectrum. Yes, you will gain loyal fans, but don't be surprised if you also gain some haters along the way. That is the true nature of leadership. You have to satisfy your core base and be willing to bear the brunt of those who don't agree with your message. The lesson here is that it doesn't pay to play it safe by going mainstream or going crazy. Just think about a niche that will place you in that sweet spot!

Rule 4: Learn the art of persuasion.
We shall be going deeper into how to use persuasion later on in this book, but for now, let us glean a few important nuggets of wisdom. Let's face it. Persuading people to join your movement isn't easy. However, there are five aspects that can help you persuade people to follow you:

- **Encouragement of dreams** – Everyone in your audience has a dream. What you need to do is understand those dreams and then encourage them to move forward with them.
- **Justification of failure** – Many of your followers will have attempted to change their lives by following other experts, but for some reason, they failed. You need to take that load of failure off them and lay the blame on their past attempts.

- **Allayment of fears** – People are looking for leaders who give them hope for the future. Instead of simply telling people not to fear, provide support and tell them stories that take their minds off the fear.
- **Confirmation of suspicions** – People usually suspect that they have the ability to change their lives, but they are looking out for leaders who will confirm this suspicion. The person who rises up to do so is the one they will follow.
- **Common enemies** – In order to grow your audience, you need to show them that you are all facing a common enemy that you need to collectively overcome. The enemy could be a philosophy, a religion, or an illness. Coming together to face a common enemy creates lasting bonds.

Rule 5: Show people that you care.
Charismatic leaders display a caring attitude toward their followers. The worst thing you can do is to create the impression that you are just interested in their wallets. Most experts feel guilty charging their audience for their services. However, one thing has made itself clear over the years – people who pay for services are more likely to take action. Secondly, as you become more successful, your time will be more

limited, which means you won't be able to interact with everyone. It simply makes sense to charge your services so that paying customers get to feel that you are invested in their success.

Rule 6: Provide value.
People have different reasons for following your movement. For some, it is a return on value. For others, it's learning opportunities or being part of a community. Avoid the tendency to define "value" for your followers, but rather let them tell you what they value from their relationship with you.

These are six rules that can help you become a charismatic leader. This will take time, but the important thing is to begin to share your message now consistently. Create super fans by polarizing your message. Be vulnerable and open. Before you know it, you will be the leader of your own tribe!

DEVELOPING A CAUSE

This is the second piece of the jigsaw puzzle necessary to create your mass movement. As a charismatic leader, you must show the people a future worth fighting for so that they can start envisioning their new lives. You need to create a cult movement with all the positives and none of the negative aspects that cults are associated with.

Rather than fear what lies ahead, you should inspire your audience to have faith in the changes that you offer to their lives. The cause must be something much larger than an individual, and as the leader, you are tasked with creating that vision.

There are four key things that can help you develop your cause:

1. Create Hope

Every mass movement in history rode on the wave of hope. By creating hope for a better future, you enable people to have the faith required to take progressive action. Without a solid vision for a better future, nobody can achieve his or her goals and dreams.

We can also observe this phenomenon in political duels, where the winners tend to offer the people an opportunity to change things while the losers focus on trying to improve what is already there.

In the initial phases of building a mass movement, you may be unsure of how to create this hope for your followers. What you need to do is ask yourself what inspired you to keep going despite all the failures of the past. It can be a simple statement that kept your vision of the future alive, but with a bit of creativity, you can make a similar statement to inspire hope in your followers.

It is important that you come up with a vision statement that resonates with the majority of the people and not just a few followers. It may be necessary to write and rewrite that vision statement until you get something that can appeal to every follower. It would be immensely helpful if your statement of hope had a personal story attached to it so that you can use it to show people just how effective it worked for you. This statement will remind your followers of the better future they have chosen to put their hope in.

2. Lead By Example

There are many people out there who want to achieve great things but they are overcome by doubt because they are yet to see someone achieve the same goal.

Prior to 1954, nobody believed it was humanly possible to run the mile in under 4 minutes. However, when Roger Bannister achieved the feat, people saw it was indeed possible. It's the same thing with every other goal.

So what does this mean for your own mass movement? If you want people to buy into your cause, you have to show them that the future they desire is achievable. You have to go ahead of them and make that vision a reality in your own life so they can believe what they previously thought was impossible. You will be able to show them tangible evidence that inspires hope in them, not just to achieve low targets, but to break records.

The result will be a change in focus from merely making money to changing lives. Of course, as people start to bear the fruits of your vision, they will pay you well. More of your followers will start becoming success stories and as word spreads, you will discover that your mass movement is growing faster than your wildest imagination.

3. Create a Group Identity

So far, you have managed to create a vision of what the future looks like. Now it's time to get your followers to identify with the movement. They need to identify why they are important in the group, otherwise, they won't feel any connection with their fellow members. Creating an identity helps people feel part of something bigger. There is great power in having a group identity.

Whenever a new follower joins your movement, it is important to bring them to the point where they can say, "I'm a _____." This creates a shift in their identity, and they instantly start to feel reborn into a new family heading toward a new future.

It is important to make sure that whatever identity you choose to create appeals to all of your members. If you are launching a new product and want to create a movement around it, you must pick a slogan that will attract your niche market. Try to figure out what kind of quote or slogan you can put on a T-shirt that your followers would want to wear. This quote will be something that every member will be proud to identify with.

4. Create a Rallying Call

Every mass movement goes through highs and lows. You are going to need a rallying cry to rouse people up during those times when doubt and unbelief sets in. Your rallying call should reignite your follower's faith in you, himself or herself, and the vision you are moving toward. So how do you do this?

Option 1: Create a mini manifesto your members can save as their smartphone or tablet background. Just take the quote or slogan that identifies your group and add your core values as a reminder of what your movement stands for.

Option 2: Create the actual manifesto. One innovative way of doing this is to look at everything that is wrong with your industry and affects customers negatively. Then use these issues to create a manifesto where you differentiate yourself from the rest of the industry. Use your manifesto to inform your members that your movement is unique and create an "Us versus Them" mentality. This manifesto can be converted into a desktop background so that your followers will see it every time they switch on their computers.

Option 3: Create a video title sequence where you have a script that rallies your members. Whenever a member hears or watches the video, they instantly know who the leader of the movement is, what the movement is about, what makes it unique, and the common vision you are all fighting for. The video doesn't have to be long - a minute will do – but it must clearly define the movement and its cause. If someone sees the video and is inspired, they will want to join. If they aren't, then life will still go on. Besides, your movement is only for true believers.

A FRESH START

The previous two chapters covered two of the things you need to build a mass movement. Now it's time to complete the puzzle by looking at the final piece – offering your followers a fresh start. Though we may be discussing this last, it is actually the most critical aspect of building your movement. Putting in place a fresh start is what determines whether you achieve a modicum of success or you end up revolutionizing the world.

If you want to understand the power behind this concept, just examine every revolutionary leader in history that has started a successful movement. They all offered their people a fresh start. They didn't approach their followers with promises of improving what was already there. They promised to provide new opportunities and break away from the past. Forget about adding new features to an existing product. We want to show you how to create something new and better!

WHY YOUR FOLLOWERS WILL REJECT IMPROVEMENT OFFERS
If you are simply interested in providing your followers with an improvement offer, be prepared for

an internal revolt. Nobody is going to buy whatever you are selling. Do you want to know why?

1. **Making Improvements is Hard** – The majority of people have tried making their lives better in the past, but for one reason or another, nothing worked. There is pain associated with such memories, and because of that, they won't want to go through the same processes again. They would rather embrace something totally new whose pain they know nothing about.

2. **Lack of Ambition** – Everybody desires something, but very few (a mere 2%) are ambitious. If you make an improvement offer, you will attract the ambitious achievers, but you will be locking out the 98% who desire change. You will lose the opportunity to make a difference.

3. **Bad Memories of the Past** – Offering an improvement forces your followers to admit their past choices were failures, and nobody likes to do so. As the charismatic leader of a mass movement, your job is to justify their failures, and only a fresh start does that.

4. **Commodity Pricing** – By offering an improvement, you are competing with other similar products in the market, and this will force prices to come down. You will have turned your vision into a mere commodity.

THE SECRET FACTOR

There is one major reason your followers will reject mere improvements. This one factor will determine whether people buy into your vision or not. This factor is STATUS.

Believe it or not, your followers will judge whether the new opportunity you are offering will bring them greater status or not. In other words, it is all a matter of self-perception rather than how others perceive you. Will your new opportunity raise their status in their own eyes or will it decrease it? This one factor determines almost all decisions we make in our lives.

If the fresh start you are offering will make a person smarter, wealthier, or more attractive, people will join your movement. But if they sense that it will reduce their status, they will be afraid to try it. There are people who have tried losing weight using several different diets, but nothing worked. If your new opportunity promises to help them lose weight, their fear level will be high because they don't want to fail again and look stupid.

However, every opportunity presents a potential status increase and status decrease. People will look at the cost of the new opportunity and try to weigh whether it is worth the risk or not. Their status may decrease initially but the final result may increase their status. Your job as the expert is to stack the potential for status increase and minimize the status decrease column.

Here are four factors that can help you increase the status potential of your product:

- Perception of increase in intelligence
- Perception of increase in power, wealth, or happiness
- Physical appearance
- Style

THE NEED FOR A FRESH START
So far we have learned why offering an improvement isn't a good idea. Now let's look at why people are drawn toward a fresh start.

1. New opportunities result in an immediate increase in status. When someone finds a new

video on YouTube, they immediately share it with their friends so everyone will know they were the first to see it. New discoveries make you look cool.

2. New opportunities allow people to leave the pain behind and move forward with a new thing. An improvement, however, forces them to disengage from past pain, and this causes a decrease in their status.

3. New opportunities enable people to embrace new dreams of their potential success. Many people are afraid of failing, and this cripples their desire to change their lives. A fresh start gives them a new dream to focus on.

4. Offering new ideas allows people the opportunity to cross over and enjoy greener pastures. An improvement simply offers them the chance to fix their own pastures, and this isn't enough to convince them to follow you.

HOW TO CREATE A NEW OPPORTUNITY

Change can only be realized once you have the right leader, the right cause, and the right opportunity. Your mass movement is now primed for changing the lives of people and making you a lot of money in the process. However, how do you create that fresh opportunity, and what do you do if you already have an existing product?

There are two approaches to creating a new opportunity:

- **Opportunity Switching**

Everyone in your target audience has tried a particular strategy to achieve a desired goal. Maybe they are on the Paleo diet to lose weight, so an opportunity switch is where you offer them a new alternative, such as Carb Cycling. If Carb Cycling has become too common, then it cannot be considered a fresh start, so you will have to create a sub-niche.

An opportunity switch relieves them from the pain they are in and infuses hope of a better future. It can involve switching from one niche to another, such as from flipping houses to selling homes on eBay. It can also involve switching between submarkets, for example, moving from selling real estate to Internet marketing. The switch can happen via e-books, webinars, or videos.

- **Opportunity Stacking**

Once you have convinced someone to switch opportunities, you have to keep adding value to their lives. Since you cannot keep switching them from one opportunity to another in perpetuity, you must stack new opportunities on top of each other to generate more sales.

For example, this book is aimed at switching you from whatever career path you are on to a different one. Once that has been accomplished, we must find new opportunities to help you move up higher. We can offer new tools, certifications, and strategies to ensure that you succeed in your new career. This is what opportunity stacking is all about.

SWITCHING OPPORTUNITIES

We have come very far, but the truth is that you haven't defined what you want to sell. It is only when you start selling something that your relationship with your audience is created, and you can then become an expert. So what's the first step?

Most people start creating new opportunities by writing books. However, this can take too long, and you need to have your message perfected first before you can write anything worth reading. So now what? How do you design an opportunity or vehicle that your followers will embrace?

Let's consider two fundamental things:
- Understanding the results people need to achieve
- Finding the right vehicle that will get people to their preferred result

STEP 1: WORK FOR FREE TO GAIN EARLY RESULTS
This may seem counterproductive to most people, but the truth is that working for free allows you to show just how much value you can offer to someone. As a newbie entrepreneur trying to launch a successful business, you will be tempted to go down the well-worn path of creating a website and videos that talk

about how great you are at what you do. The problem with this approach is that no one wants to hear you brag about your skills, and secondly, you haven't proven to anyone that your expertise is of value.

What you need to do is identify at least one entrepreneur whom you would wish to work with and offer your services to them for free. The aim here is to serve others and in the process, get them to see that your expertise is worth paying for. Instead of going through the whole process of trying to convince people that they should pay you for what you are offering, first provide that service for free and let your results speak for themselves.

Don't forget to collect as many testimonials and success stories as possible to share with your potential audience. Your target clients will see how you helped others and they will be drawn to your business.

STEP 2: CREATE YOUR VEHICLE
Where can you find clients and how do you design the right vehicle to teach them? Here is a simple process that is quite effective.

- **Define your sub-market and what you intend to do for them.** This can be summarized in one single statement that clarifies who your message is meant to serve and what fresh opportunity you intend to avail. For example, use a statement like: "I am going to teach *freelance writers* how to *generate income by incorporating SEO into their writing*."

- **Create an attractive headline for your target customers**. A great way to do this is by focusing on your deliverables. A good format would look like this:

    How to (customer's desired result) without (customer's greatest fear)

    If you want to teach people how to flip houses online, your headline would be:

    "How to Generate $5k in One Weekend by Flipping a House Online Without a Bank Loan"

- **Generate curiosity to get people to leave their current vehicle and get into yours.** There are five different hooks you can use to entice your customers to switch opportunities.

Let's assume that your niche is helping people to lose weight via ketosis:

1) **Unknown but makes a big difference**. Your hook will be, "Ever heard of ketosis? Most people aren't aware of it but it's pretty effective in boosting energy levels and shedding pounds."
2) **Known but poorly understood**. Your hook will be, "Cutting carbs is popular right now. Yes, we should avoid refined sugar, but lowering carb intake isn't responsible for weight loss. It's the ketosis! As long as you drink ketones, you can still eat your carbs."
3) **Major changes happening**. Your hook will be, "Do you suffer from excessive cravings due to your diet? We now offer new ketones that induce ketosis immediately, stop cravings, and guarantee weight loss. Major changes are happening!"
4) **Crystal ball angle**. Your hook will be, "Have you been counting calories with no actual loss in weight? Studies show that reducing carb intake is useless in helping the average person stay in

ketosis. The future of low-carb dieting is in drinking ketones directly."
5) **Sticking to the basics**. Your hook will be, "Today's diets are simply too complicated for the average person. They force you to count every morsel consumed and every second you work out. We stick to the basics – Just chug a ketone drink when you wake up and before bed, maintain a daily carb intake lower than 20 grams, and you're done!"

What you need to take note of is that every hook goes against conventional market norms. Just pick the one that will work best for you when you finally create your masterclass.

STEP 3: ASK CUSTOMERS WHAT THEY DESIRE
One thing you need to remember is that customers don't purchase their needs, they purchase their wants. This means that on top of offering them a new opportunity, you also have to identify what their exact wants are within that opportunity. There are three steps you need to follow:

1) Determine the right market
2) Ask customers what their wants are
3) Provide them

For example, you can ask customers a single question as part of your webpage survey, such as, "What's the one question you need answered about_____?"

To entice people to participate, you can offer them a free ticket to your masterclass. Tell everyone about the survey, starting with your family and friends. Then reach out to other potential customers by browsing through forums, online communities, and social media groups that are related to the sub-market you are in. Introduce yourself and interact with people for about two weeks before you can start asking them to participate in your survey.

Once you achieve 100 responses to your survey, you will discover that there are about 10 questions that keep popping up. Take these 10 questions and make them the titles for the modules you will create for your masterclass. Research the answers to each question in order to deliver a great master class. Your audience will enjoy your teachings because you will be providing them with precisely what they wanted.

When that is done, go one step further and convert every question that was submitted in the survey into a bullet point. Each question provides insight into what customers want to know, and this gives you a hint of what to include in your sales letters, emails, ads, and webinars. If you like, you can now go ahead and use all the information you have collected to create a book.

STEP 4: TEACH YOUR MASTERCLASS
This should be simple because all you need is to create a group on Facebook and use Facebook Live. The membership site can come later on, but for now, you can use the group to provide information about the timings and dates of your webinars.

This is the end of Part I of the book. We have so far seen the kind of service you can offer to your customers. Now that they know there is value in your expertise, get ready to learn how to monetize your services.

PART II: CREATING BELIEF

The previous section talked about becoming a leader and creating a mass movement. Now we shall look at how to persuade people to believe your message and your vision through storytelling.

THE ONE BIG THING

What is that one thing that, if you were to get your customers to believe, would eliminate every objection they have toward your message? The truth is that if you focus on getting your customers to believe in several different things about your product, you stand less chance of making a sale. This is the challenge you now face when trying to sell your product. There is only one big belief that you have to eliminate before all the other smaller customer objections fall by the wayside.

Are you familiar with logic arguments? For example:

If you are reading this book, then you are quite intelligent.
You are reading this book.
Therefore, you are quite intelligent.

Logic arguments are all around us, even in sports and politics. This is what makes it so difficult to argue with a person who holds a particular belief. You may try to convince them of other beliefs, but as long as that major belief is still standing, you cannot win.

So what is your big thing statement? What is that one statement that you can make to get your audience to believe you? Here is an example of such a statement:

If I am able to make my customers believe that (the new opportunity I am offering) is critical to (their business success) and can only be attained via (my particular process), then every other objection and concern is rendered immaterial and they must pay me money.

What such a statement does is that it gets a customer to believe that once they get their hands on whatever you are offering, which is only available from you, they will be successful. There is no other avenue to success other than by buying from you.

The important thing to note here is that your statement must be true. If what you are offering is not at all critical, or is available elsewhere, or the opportunity is not new, then you will be found out. Nobody is going to believe you and you will not make any money. Just make sure that your big statement is true and works.

BRIDGING THE EMOTIONAL DIVIDE

Building a mass movement with you as the leader is akin to selling the people a new opportunity. You are trying to show them that joining your movement is worth it, so you have to convince them to buy into your vision. However, this is where most experts get it wrong. They focus so much on using facts and logic to sell something instead of trying to create an emotional connection between the people and the idea.

If you want to make your job easier, you have to lead them toward a specific conclusion rather than just giving them a ready-made answer. This is possible if you tell them a great story. The aim of the story is to make them believe that the conclusion they came up with is their own, thus allowing them to make their own buying decision. If you can do this successfully, the product will practically sell itself. This concept is known as an Epiphany Bridge.

An Epiphany Bridge is a simple story that allows people to experience the same emotions that YOU felt when you discovered the opportunity you are presenting them. In other words, you are trying to transmit your passion about the opportunity on offer by telling your customers about your amazing experience.

Think of the "aha" moment that you had when you first identified this new opportunity. You must have felt so excited that you couldn't stop talking or reading about it. You wanted to absorb everything about the topic and understand the fundamental and technical concept behind it. Ultimately, you went from an emotional bond to being logically sold.

Since you are passionate about the idea, you cannot resist the urge to share what you have learned with the world. But this is where most people mess up. They flip the sequence around by trying to use logic to convince people to buy into the new opportunity, assuming that this will trigger an emotional connection. You will be shocked when you discover that people don't feel the same way about the opportunity like you do.

So where did you go wrong? Here's what happened. You started using logic to sell instead of using emotions! You started speaking a language that your customers couldn't understand, something we refer to as "Technobabble." If people cannot emotionally connect to whatever you are offering, you won't make any sales.

That is why you need to be an effective storyteller. The Epiphany Bridge about how excited you felt about the new opportunity is what will sell your idea. Once the emotional aspect has been established, then you can start logically justifying why the new opportunity is a good idea. Your story will bridge the gap between emotions and logic.

HOW TO TELL A GOOD STORY
There are times when two different people will narrate to you the exact same experience they went through, but one story will appear way more captivating than the other. Why is that? How come one person can tell a more engaging story than another?

The reasons may be many, but all you need are a few things to spice up any story. The first thing is oversimplification. Believe it or not, but the majority of people can only pay attention to your story if you talk to them at a 3rd-grade level. This is difficult for most of us because we want to appear intelligent and sophisticated, so we incorporate big words into our stories. This makes it hard for the audience to digest your information and you lose your influence over them.

So what if you have a complicated idea that you want to communicate to your audience? You simply break it down into everyday language by incorporating the phrase "kinda like." For example, if you are talking about a complex topic like ketones and how they benefit the body, you could say:

It is important to drink ketones. But what are these ketones? Ketones are kinda like tiny motivational speakers that move through the body increasing your energy levels and giving you an awesome feeling.

All you have to do is use the phrase "kinda like" to bridge the gap between your vague concept and something they already understand. This is how you become an effective and entertaining storyteller.

IT'S ALL ABOUT THEIR FEELINGS
If you want people to connect better with your ideas, you have to add more emotions to your story. Just look at some of the biggest blockbusters from Hollywood. You will notice that instead of the character just telling us directly what happened to them during their childhood, we will be taken into a flashback scene depicting everything they went through. We will see, hear, and experience everything they did. Setting up a scene and explaining emotions is the best way to get your audience to feel your feelings.

As you explain your epiphany, make sure that you infuse every emotion you felt, not by merely telling the audience, but by describing in vivid details what you went through. If you can get your audience to share your experiences at an emotional level, they will buy anything you sell them.

STRUCTURING YOUR STORY

It's time for us now to look at how to structure a good story. Selling a story is a great way to excite people about something, but without a proper structure, it will be a hit-or-miss affair. Understanding good story structure will help you create an appropriate environment for your audience to experience their own epiphanies.

KEEP IT SIMPLE, STUPID
One thing you should remember is that the best stories are always simple. Though they may be complex on the outside, the core is quite simple. There are three elements that form the plot of a good story. They are:

- Character
- Desire
- Conflict

Every book, movie, or play will have these basic elements. There has to be a fascinating character that has a compelling desire to achieve a goal against what seem like insurmountable odds.

Let's try to create a story based on you and your epiphany. The character is you, so that part is easy. So what desire pushed you to begin your journey? Write down what you wanted to achieve. You must have experienced a conflict, so what was it? Write that down as well. There you go! You have your plot in mind and all you need to do now is write it down. For example:

There was once a man named John Black, whose desire was to provide for his young family without being forced to work a 9 to 5 job. He came up with the idea of starting an online company that sells writing services to clients all over the world. However, the cost of Google ads skyrocketed, and his small business went bust overnight.

Character: John Black
Desire: To provide financially for his young family
Conflict: Cost of Google ads skyrocketed and his business went bust

There you have it. You open with a plot statement that paints the whole picture within seconds. If you want to add more details after that, you can still do so. It's up to you. Let's dig deeper into the individual elements.

1. **The Character**

The beginning of every story is all about building a rapport with the main character. This enables the audience to care about the character throughout the story. This can be achieved by defining the character's identity either as a victim; in jeopardy; likable; funny; or powerful. Don't forget to introduce some weaknesses in the character to gain more rapport with the audience.

2. **Desire**

The character in your story must either be moving toward pleasure or is running away from pain. It is this desire that drives them to achieve their goal. The character moves toward pain because they want to win something (love, money, fame, etc.) or retrieve something valuable. They may also be running from past pain in order to escape from the thing that is causing their pain or stop a bad event from occurring.

The hero in your story should be on a two-fold journey: to achieve some goal, or to transform their identity. In most cases, we focus a lot on the hero achieving something great, but the truth is that it is more important for the character to be transformed into someone greater than before. This may mean even sacrificing their goal just to create a new identity and belief.

3. **The Conflict**

The goal is represented by the desire, but the emotional connection is only forged through the conflict the character faces as they move toward that goal. The audience will only care if the odds are stacked against the character, so as the storyteller, you shouldn't make it an easy journey for the hero of the story. Every good story must have five conflict turning points:

- **New opportunity** – Once you have painted a picture of their past, there has to be some event that forces the character to leave where they are and begin their journey. They are chasing a new opportunity that seems like a good idea initially.
- **Modifying the plan** – Their initial goal will then change into a specific objective that motivates the character. This will lead to progress until the next turning point.
- **No turning back** – So far, the character has had the option of going back, but at this point, he must choose to forget what is behind and move forward. The stakes are raised and this leads him to the next turning point.
- **The big setback** – The character experiences an event that makes his journey seem hopeless.

However, there is a tiny glimmer of hope, and with only a single option left, he chooses to take it. This leads to the final turning point.
- **The climax** – The character must go through the biggest hurdle of their journey in order to achieve their desire and transform their life. After this comes the aftermath, where we see the character living a new life.

This is the formula every great movie has used and mastering it will help you in whatever you choose to do in your life.

SCRIPTING YOUR EPIPHANY BRIDGE STORIES

We are now in a good position to begin creating awesome stories for your Epiphany Bridge script. This is linked to the way we developed our character in the previous section. It is important that you become well acquainted with this script because it will help you build your mass movement.

There are eight sections that are critical to developing your script. Every section has a question attached to it, and by answering that question, the story will be writing itself. Treat the eight sections as a progression where one leads seamlessly into the other. Here are the eight sections that will provide you with a framework for telling any story:

1. **The Backstory – What about your past experiences can help us relate to your journey?**

Your audience will look at you as an expert and start doubting whether they have what it takes to get to where you are. This is why your backstory is important. You need to tell people about the hard circumstances you went through before you began your journey. Show them that, once upon a time, you were also exactly where they are now. This will build their faith in their abilities and help them move toward their dreams.

2. Your Desires – What do you feel compelled to accomplish?

Remember the three basic elements we talked about in the previous chapter? You need to get your audience to think about what their inner desires are. However, the majority of people aren't even aware that there are two kinds of conflicts that prevent them from getting their desires: surface (external) resistance and deeper (internal) resistance.

External resistance is the primary motivator of the character's first journey. It is usually dependent on your desire and is linked to a specific goal: winning, retrieving, escaping, or stopping. We learned about these four goals earlier in the book. The important thing to note is that people are likely to share what their external problems are without realizing they are not the actual issue. For example, a person may say, "I want to lose a few pounds, but I'm finding it difficult to stop eating carbs."

So what is the real issue then? There is an internal resistance that we all have to deal with. This is linked to the transformation that we all seek in our lives. The character in the story must move past their fear and onto boldness. It can be difficult to identify your internal conflict and share it with your audience because this will force you to show your vulnerability. However, it is also a powerful way to build rapport with the audience because they too struggle with similar issues.

To identify your internal struggle, just take your external struggle and ask "Why" about six times. At the end of it all, the answer you come up with will be linked to either love or status. It is more important for the audience to see how you managed to overcome your internal struggles even if you are still working on the external one.

3. **The Wall – Can you identify the wall that was preventing you from achieving success within your old/current opportunity?**

The members of your audience can only be willing to try a new opportunity with you if their current or past opportunities failed to get them to their destination. The wall is something that frustrates you as you attempt to achieve your goals or desires. For your audience to experience an epiphany at this point, you have to describe to them your own personal fears, hopelessness, and frustrations so that they can see the benefit of taking a new path.

4. The Epiphany – Can you identify your epiphany experience and the new opportunity?

Your epiphany is the point in your life where you discover that there is a better path than the one you are currently on. It can come via a person, an idea, or a breakthrough in a conflict. This epiphany must lead to the realization a new vehicle to get you to your goals.

5. The Plan – How do you intend to accomplish your desire?

You need to come up with a step-by-step plan for reaching your goals. Inevitably, you will experience some obstacles, which just adds greater emotion into the story. Remember that the audience doesn't connect to the character in the story simply because they have a desire; it is the conflict that triggers emotions.

6. The Conflict – Can you explain the conflict you experienced on your journey?

There is always a conflict that will be faced, and a decision must be made to keep moving forward or turn back. Most people lack the faith necessary to take action on their epiphany. However, this time things will be different because you will decide to make it a do-or-die affair. This is where you inspire your audience to also do the same. In every good story, once the central character chooses to risk it all and move forward, they face great challenges. Describe your conflicts in a way that shows how hopeless your situation was until something shifted and you decided to give it one more shot.

7. **The Accomplishment – What was the ultimate result?**

Share what happened in the end. You either succeeded in accomplishing your desires or you didn't.

8. **The Transformation – Can you explain your transformation experience?**

The transformation process leads you to become a new person with new beliefs. It is at this point that your inner conflicts are resolved and former belief patterns are broken. This is the ultimate aim of an Epiphany Bridge story.

YOUR ORIGIN STORY

In one of the previous chapters of the book, we talked about The One Big Thing that you have to get your audience to believe if they are to follow you. This statement is reinforced by what we refer to as your "origin story."

What you need to do now is take a look at your origin story and then use it to answer the eight critical questions we have just highlighted above. Your origin story is crucial for converting sales so ensure that you dedicate enough time and effort to develop it well. If your audience reads your Epiphany Bridge story, they should believe that your new opportunity is the only way to achieve success, and they will want to buy from you.

FALSE MINDSETS

We all have false beliefs, especially about any new opportunities we encounter. A false mindset forms the basis of our beliefs all the way from birth, and we create stories to justify why we believe what we believe. What we don't realize is that these false beliefs are preventing us from moving forward with our lives.

The moment you try to convince someone to buy a new opportunity, their mindset kicks in and they begin to look at why that opportunity won't help them. These false beliefs are created through past experiences that could be either negative or positive. The experience causes your mind to create a supporting story, and that story is converted into a belief. This is why it is possible to have two people go through the same thing but have different beliefs. It's all about the story they created around that experience. The good news is that these false beliefs can be broken.

How False Beliefs Work

- Step 1: Think of any false beliefs that your customers could have regarding the new opportunity you are offering. For example, you may be offering a weight loss opportunity, so a false belief could be:

"If I attempt to drop a few pounds, I will not feel happy."

- Step 2: Try to determine the experience that created the false belief. For example, it could be that they attempted to lose some weight in the past, but because they had to eliminate the carbs, they ended up hating the diet.

- Step 3: Figure out the story that they have created to prevent them from grabbing the new opportunity. For example, the person's story could be that they have to forego what they enjoy just to lose some weight.

- Step 4: Create an epiphany story, whether personal or based on someone else's life, to show your customer that you share a belief similar to theirs, but now that you have created a new story, that false belief pattern has been replaced. For example:

"I too believed that losing weight involved a lot of misery. However, I came to learn about a

> new diet that didn't involve eliminating carbs at all."

This is truly an exciting process that allows you to see how powerful a story can be when trying to change a person's beliefs. The story will unravel the truth, and once the customer adopts a new belief, they will grab the new opportunity.

The best thing to do right now is to start building a list of epiphany stories for every potential false belief your customers may have regarding the new opportunity you're offering. List 10-20 false beliefs and run them through the four steps outlined above. When the right time comes, you will have an inventory of stories to inspire them to buy your products or services.

THREE BELIEF ROADBLOCKS

It would be great if you could offer a prospect a new opportunity, tell them your epiphany story, help them adopt a new belief, and snag yourself a lifetime customer. However, this is not always the case. There are times when the customer will eliminate the big false belief but then come up with many other concerns.

Based on our experience, there are generally three major categories of beliefs that prevent a customer from taking up a new opportunity:

- Beliefs about the new opportunity
- Inner beliefs regarding their ability to take action
- External beliefs regarding forces outside their control, e.g. the economy or time

What you need to do is come up with false beliefs that may fall under each of these categories. Since you followed the advice given in the previous chapter, you already have a list of about 10-20 false beliefs that can fall under these categories.

Create three columns: one for vehicle, the next for inner beliefs, and the last one for external beliefs.

Examine each false belief, and as you classify them, determine which one is the most critical belief under each category. This core belief should be at the top of the column.

Let's look at a brief example.

You begin by presenting your opportunity headline:

How to Lose 30 Pounds in 30 Days without Eliminating Carbs from Your Diet

Then you present the big thing statement you created in chapter 5:

If I am able to make my customers believe that (my new dieting technique) is critical to (their weight loss success) and can only be attained via (my dieting process X), then every other objection and concern is rendered immaterial and they must pay me money.

At this point, you tell them your epiphany story to get them to want to use your technique to lose weight. But after their major false belief is eliminated, the other concerns crop up. What you need to do is use your Epiphany Bridge stories to deal with every false belief in whatever category it comes up in. For example:

- **False belief about the new opportunity** – "Your new diet technique seems great, but I don't see how it will work in my case." Handle this by telling them a story of how you managed to use the same dieting technique with people of various ages, sizes, occupations, and etc. The aim is to get the customer to see that they can model someone else's success.

- **Inner false beliefs** – "I love the new diet technique but it seems a bit too complicated for me." Tell them a story of how a past client, who had minimal education and absolutely no experience with diets, was able to understand the new technique and lose weight.

- **External beliefs** – "OK. I may be able to do this new diet, but I don't know where I would get the time for it." You will whip out a story of how a busy mom with five kids was able to use the diet to lose weight successfully without compromising her work.

See how simple that was? Now you move onto the next critical step. You have false beliefs and epiphany stories that can break each one of them. You can use all the information you have to create a list of "secrets" to arouse the curiosity of your customers. Remember that curiosity sells, so here is an example of how to rewrite the false beliefs and epiphany stories into secrets.

Secret 1: How You Can Have a Body Like Jessica Biel in Just 30 Days!

Secret 2: How to Lose Weight Even If You Have Never Gone on a Diet Before!

Secret 3: How to Achieve your Weight Loss Goals By Spending Just 15 Minutes a Day Doing This!

You now have all you need to create an effective sales presentation, which we will talk about in the next part of the book. All along you have been working toward getting people to believe in your new opportunity and join your mass movement. In order to achieve this, you had to eliminate that one major false belief as well as any other concerns they might have. Whatever false mindsets they had have been replaced by new beliefs. Now that they are primed and ready to take action, let's look at how you can finally make that sale.

PART III: YOUR CALL OF DUTY

The first two parts of this book covered how to create a mass movement and how to create new beliefs for your followers. This section is all about sales. The truth is that if you believe that what you are offering is of benefit, you have a moral duty to serve people with it.

You are going to learn some strategies for converting your audience into paying customers. Selling your product or service to the masses within a short window of time is a skill you can master, so if you want your message to bring in cold, hard cash, prepare to learn some amazing tactics here.

THE PREMIUM OFFER

One of the first things you need to do before you sell anything is to create an offer that customers cannot resist. You want to make sure that when you finish your presentation, your product sells. You essentially come up with a list of all the benefits the customer is guaranteed to receive, including bonuses, when they buy your product.

The first thing you need to do is note down everything you can do for your customer to help them achieve their goal. This is a brainstorming session, so let your creativity flow, as outrageous as some ideas may seem.

The next step is to take the best ideas from your brainstorming session and create a list of deliverables that can fit into your pricing scheme. Every deliverable has a specific value, so you should aim at showing the customer that the total value of the offer is 10 times more valuable than what you are asking them to pay.

There are six elements that can help you create a premium offer:

1. **Your Masterclass**

This should be first on your offer list. It includes the teachings that your beta customers will learn during the free masterclass. Once you hold that first free class, every successive class should charge a fee and be more detailed in terms of content being offered. If not, you will find yourself repeating content from the masterclass.

2. **The Tools**

These are the things that you offer to participants of your masterclass to make their learning easier. It can be a simple template or checklist, or complex software. It may seem like a good idea to offer more training as part of your premium list, but participants may associate this with a greater workload. You are better off sticking with things like cheat sheets, scripts, schedules, or templates. Participants tend to view your tools as more valuable than a paid masterclass, so ensure that you put enough thought into this.

3. **Deliverable 1**

This is linked to the vehicle or opportunity on offer. You need to consider which false beliefs your customers may have regarding the new opportunity you are offering. If there is anything that is preventing them from seeing this opportunity as a perfect fit for them, you need to do something to change that perception. You can create a case study video or booklet where you share some success stories of people who have used the vehicle to achieve their goals. This product then becomes a deliverable.

4. **Deliverable 2**

This is linked to the customer's inner struggle. Once you have convinced them that the opportunity is perfect for them, you have to tackle any negative inner beliefs they have regarding their ability to succeed. This means you have to come up with a deliverable that will assist them in overcoming any personal false beliefs. You may have to train them on a few specific techniques that aren't part of your masterclass.

5. **Deliverable 3**

This is linked to the customer's external struggle and is usually the final hurdle that you have to overcome to get them to buy the product. They may believe that the opportunity is perfect and that they are able to succeed, but they fear that external forces will interfere with their chances of success. Think of anything that is beyond their control that may prevent them from succeeding and identify a deliverable that will minimize or eliminate it.

6. Bonus offer

This is an urgent and scarce offer that is meant to entice your customers to sign up for your new opportunity. You should offer a special discount or product for only those people who sign up before a specific deadline. You can also make a special offer to the first 50 people who buy your product.

Now that you have created a list of premium offers for your customers, you can use it to reel them in and start making sales. Next, we look at how to create a script for presenting and selling your premium offer.

THE PERFECT PRESENTATION

The script that you are going to create in this chapter can work with a variety of selling situations, such as webinars, teleseminars, stage presentations, video sales letters, email sequences, etc.

For now, we shall break the script process down and then go into greater details in the next three chapters. Keep in mind that the main objective is to get your audience to believe in just ONE THING - That one thing that, if you were to get your customers to believe, would eliminate every objection they have toward your message. Trying to get them to believe in more than one thing will hurt your sales.

The script you are about to learn is fluid but every component is critical. It contains three main sections.

Section 1: Building Rapport
This is the introductory section of your script and includes the welcome message. The goal is to trigger the curiosity of participants, excite them, and build a rapport. Don't forget that your introduction should be where you begin persuading people, so don't waste it.

Section 2: Eliminating the One Thing
The second step is to identify that one belief that needs to be knocked down as well as to tell the audience the epiphany story that opened your eyes to the opportunity.

Section 3: Breaking the Three Core False Beliefs
This is where you present your content. You identify the core false beliefs that center on the vehicle, internal beliefs, and external beliefs. We already talked about these earlier, so all you have to do is find appropriate epiphany stories that will help break every false belief the audience has. Then go ahead and begin to rebuild their mindset with the truth.

Don't view this step as trying to get the audience to believe something new. Just focus on eliminating those false beliefs that they have regarding your new opportunity and they will want to follow you.

Section 4: Making the Offer
Now you are ready to transition from teaching the audience to selling your product. There is a specific format that we will share with you that has proven to be very effective in persuading people to grab your offer in order to achieve their goals.

That was just an overview of what the perfect presentation is all about. Once you have learned the structure, you will be able to use it seamlessly. The most important thing is to be aware of the objectives each section has. This is what we will cover in the chapters ahead.

PUTTING YOUR SCRIPT TOGETHER

Now that you are in possession of all pieces that form the foundation of your script, it's time to go through the entire process of writing your script. This is where you learn how to start and complete your presentation.

You can use Keynote or PowerPoint to create your presentation, and this means you will have to create slides. In case your presentation is a sequence of emails rather than a webinar, you can still incorporate slides to remind yourself of the content that you have to cover in every phase.

There are generally two ways of scripting your webinar, depending on personal preference. You can either create a script composed of bullet points on a slide, or you can write down the entire script and just read everything. Just make sure you choose a format that you are personally comfortable with. However, since you are learning how to create a script for the first time, it is probably best that you just write everything down. Once you become accustomed to delivering a live webinar, you can then use bullet points.

Let's move over to the scripting process.

INTRODUCING THE PRESENTATION
Usually, the introduction requires 5-10 minutes for a regular webinar, but for other selling environments, it should take less time. This is the part where you excite the audience and build rapport.

There are nine steps, or slides, that form the introduction:

Step 1: The Title Slide
This is what the audience will see the moment they access the live webinar or replay, so it has to arouse their curiosity. A good example would be:

> "Hello, everyone! Welcome to this webinar. My name is _____ and today you are going to learn how to lose 30 pounds in 30 days without eliminating carbs from your diet."

Step 2: Building Rapport
Earlier in the book, we talked about how to persuade people by encouraging their dreams, justifying their failures, allaying their fears, confirming their suspicions, and disparaging their enemies. Here is an example of what to say to build rapport:

- Justifying their failures – "I know that most of you have attended many other webinars in the past. I just want to say that if you didn't manage to achieve ___ in previous attempts, don't blame yourself. All the information swirling out there can be quite confusing at times, and information overload can be detrimental to your success. Don't worry about that."
- Allaying their fears – "You may have convinced yourself that _____ cannot help you succeed. Don't be afraid. You will succeed. All you need is someone who can explain to you what you need to do."
- Disparaging their enemies – "Large corporations will tell you that you cannot achieve success without a college degree or venture capital. That's not true. They know why they keep pushing that line, and it's wrong."
- Confirming their suspicions – "You may have considered the fact that banks and the government actually want to see you fail, and this is 100% true. Your success doesn't benefit them at all! They are more interested in drowning you in debt. We, on the other hand, are interested in seeing you succeed and living your dream life."

- Encouraging their dreams – "That is why we are here. I want to see you achieve your dream and impact the world, and in this webinar, I will demonstrate how you can do that."

Step 3: Presenting a New Opportunity
This slide is what the audience will use to determine whether the webinar is worth it, which is why you need to explain the goals of the presentation here. Those who realize their goals are incompatible with yours will leave at this point. Try to be as inclusive as possible so that everyone sees how the new opportunity will benefit them.

"The goal of this presentation is to help beginners to _____, while providing those with greater experience with _____."

Step 4: The Big Obstacle
Remember the sentence you created earlier that said:

If I am able to make my customers believe that (new dieting technique) is critical to (their weight loss success) and can only be attained via (my dieting process X), then every other objection and concern is rendered immaterial.

In this slide, you show the audience the big obstacle and convince them that the ONLY way for them to attain their desire is through your new opportunity.

Step 5: Position Yourself as an Expert
Your audience needs to believe someone who has the experience and skills necessary to achieve results is teaching them. Just give them a brief backstory and the internal and external results you achieved.

Step 6: Tell Your Epiphany Story
Reveal to your audience how you first learned of the new opportunity and became convinced that it would lead you to your success. The aim here is to lead them to have an "Aha" moment for their own situation.

Step 7: Make Your Story Relatable
Some people may find your epiphany tale a bit irrelevant to their situation, which means you have to reframe your story to fit their circumstances. Tell them how the traditional method works and then explain to them why the old system is difficult and confusing. Then describe to them how your new opportunity is easier and better.

Step 8: Evidence/Case Study
Include a case study or example of someone who has succeeded using your product.

"Yes, this system works. Let me tell you about Allan, who attended a previous webinar and has transformed his life within 5 short months!"

Step 9: The Transition
Though your audience is now excited, their false beliefs are bound to start popping into their minds once you mention your new opportunity. What you need to do now is transition to providing content that breaks false beliefs and replaces them with new thought patterns. Remember the three secrets you created earlier? This is where you introduce them to your audience as a way to counteract the biggest three false beliefs they have about your new opportunity.

- *Secret 1: How You Can Have a Body Like Jessica Biel in Just 30 Days!*

- *Secret 2: How to Lose Weight Even If You Have Never Gone on a Diet Before!*

- *Secret 3: How to Achieve your Weight Loss Goals by Spending Just 15 Minutes a Day Doing This!*

What a rollercoaster ride that has been! But that was just the introduction part of your presentation. Now it's time to deliver actual content.

HOW TO BREAK AND REBUILD BELIEF PATTERNS

As you now start transitioning into delivering actual content, you will try to take on the persona of a teacher. Wrong move! The presentation is not meant to teach but to inspire the audience to take the necessary action. You should focus on breaking false beliefs and building new belief patterns. Teaching only comes AFTER you have sold your product.

If you try to teach during the webinar, you will kill your sales. You may have created an awesome product that has the potential of changing lives, but you'd be surprised by how many people simply attend a webinar, learn all the new stuff they can, and walk away without buying anything. Not only will you lose money, but the participants who behave this way never manage to change their lives using your content!

There is something that happens when a person buys a product that is meant to change their life. It forces them to make a commitment to take action and their chances of success skyrocket. For those who listen to a teaching but never financially invest in the product, nothing ever changes. This is why you should not teach during your presentation. You will be crippling your audience by giving them free content. Just focus on inspiring them to break false beliefs and adopt empowering ones.

The steps continue from the previous chapter.

Step 10: Just State the First Secret
Tell the audience the first secret, which is related to the vehicle/new opportunity.

Secret 1: How You Can Have a Body Like Jessica Biel in Just 30 Days!

Then quickly transition into the subsequent slide. Say something like, "Now here is a story..."

Step 11: Tell Them Your Epiphany Story
The first false belief is linked to people doubting whether your new opportunity will really work. Tell them an epiphany story that will clarify this new opportunity and eliminate this false belief. The goal is to help them come to their own epiphany moment.

Step 12: Show Them the Results of Others
When your audience hears your story, they might think that the new opportunity worked for you because you are different from them. However, if you

present a success story from an ordinary Joe whom they can resonate with, they will see that it's possible for them as well.

Step 13: Eliminate Related Beliefs

People don't just have one false belief; they have several. There is a list of 10-20 false beliefs that you compiled earlier in the chapter on False Mindsets. These false beliefs were all about the new opportunity you are offering. It's time to whip out that list and break each and every one of them. Take as much time as you want to explain to your audience, using short epiphany stories, why their objections are misguided, until there is no resistance any more.

Step 14: Reaffirm the Secret as an Indisputable Truth

Now that the past beliefs have been proven to be false, it's time to install a new belief. Simply restate Secret 1 as truth, like this: "So now you have learned how you can have a body like Jessica Biel in just 30 days. Isn't that great?"

Step 15 – 24: Repeat Steps 10 through 14 for Secret 2 and 3

You have covered Secret 1 from steps 10 to 14, so now you have to do the same for Secrets 2 and 3. This will provide additional content for your presentation.

What you are essentially doing here is triggering a shift in the paradigm of your audience. You are helping them overcome their doubts about the new opportunity as well as themselves. It may take you up to an hour to break every false belief, but once you do, that big obstacle will tumble down. You will have transitioned from a teacher of strategies to a giver of hope, and your audience will thank you by choosing to join your mass movement.

Step 25: Transitioning to Making the Sale
Now you will begin to move from providing content to closing the deal. This can be a bit stressful for some, but there are a few techniques that can help you solidify the ideas you have imparted and get them to take action. Go through your three secrets and break everything down so that they are able to connect their own dots. Describe to them how following Secret 1, doing what you showed them in Secret 2, and using the tactics in Secret 3 will put them in a great position to achieve their goals. If they see how all the dots connect, they will agree to buy your product.

In case you are dealing with a stage presentation, it is easier to watch the audience's response as you transition to making a sale. Those who nod in agreement are usually the first ones to rush to buy the product. However, you have the opportunity of asking the rest of the audience questions in order to address any concerns. You cannot do this with a webinar, which means you must make sure you gather and address as many false beliefs as possible within that presentation.

Step 26: The Big Question
This is the part of the webinar where you reveal to the audience your offer and close the deal. For most people, this is the most nerve-wracking part. You may show signs of hesitation in your body language and voice, but fortunately, there is a way to smoothen this transition process. All you have to say is:

"Can you answer one question ... "

See how simple that is? You take the pressure off yourself and this helps you make a smooth transition. Now you can ask them a couple of questions like:

"Are you excited about the stuff we just learned about?"
"Are you feeling a bit overwhelmed by all the content we have covered?"

At this point, you can show them a funny picture of someone who appears to be overwhelmed or something. Explain to them that it isn't possible to learn everything in a presentation that lasts only one hour, though you tried your best. Tell them about the special package available to those who want to take advantage of the unique new opportunity.

Then ASK them for their permission before you share the details of the package.

"Hey, guys. Do you mind if I take the next 10 minutes sharing with you the details of one very unique offer I have to help you _____?"

If you are on stage, you can proceed if you the audience says yes or people nod their heads. This will give you the confidence to start selling. If people stay silent or don't nod, just ask them for permission to explain the benefits of the special package first. One thing is for sure: if you stick to this script from start to finish, the audience is going to give you the permission to introduce the offer.

THE SECRET WEAPON

There is a secret weapon that, if used correctly, has the power to give you a 50% closing rate for every presentation you make. Whether it's a live stage presentation or a webinar, this thing will boost you sales every single time. It is known as the stack.

What you need to keep in mind is that the audience will only remember what you showed them last. The problem with most presentations is that they place too much emphasis on the offer itself, followed by bonuses, and finally a call-to-action. This means that the audience will only remember the final bonus that was mentioned, and if the price doesn't match what they remember, they will refuse to buy.

A stack is a series of slides that are arranged in a way that ensures the audience gets to see everything on offer, including the total value of the offer. This allows them to associate the price being charged with EVERYTHING that you are offering, not just the last thing they remember.

Let's go through every individual slide that you will use to create your stack. Just as before, the steps are a continuation from the previous chapter.

Step 27: What You Get
This slide should show an image that represents the content of the course. Tell the audience that an immediate investment will result in instant admission into your masterclass.

Step 28: Overview of Deliverables
Quickly recap every weekly module on offer. Don't overwhelm people with details. Just give an overview and then transition to case studies.

Step 29: Present Three Case Studies
Introduce three people from your beta group and describe their success stories.

Step 30: Be All-Inclusive
Many people disregard case studies because they don't see the similarities between them and the people who have succeeded. They believe that the person's success was due to where they live or the career they are in. Make an all-inclusive statement that draws in everyone. For example:

> "This opportunity will work for those who want to lose 100 pounds, people who only want to drop five pounds, or those interested in building muscle."

Step 31: Eliminate the Biggest Excuse

There is always one big excuse why people don't take immediate action. Tackle it from the get-go in order to remove it from the minds of your audience. For example, the biggest excuse for not exercising is that there simply isn't enough time. Tell them:

> "You may be thinking that you can't take action because_____. That's a wrong belief that will keep you from success, and here's why..."

Step 32: The First Stack Slide

Show them the first slide containing your 6-week masterclass and the item on offer, as well as its value.

> "By signing up, you get immediate access to a 6-week masterclass with a total value of $_____."

Step 33: The Tools

Tell your audience about the tools you have created to make their work easier, for example, templates, checklists, software, schedules, etc. Just mention them rather than overwhelming people with too many details.

Step 34: Make the Offer Irresistible

Tell the audience how they will actually save money by investing in your product.

Step 35: Explain the Problem Solved
Describe how the tool you are offering helped you overcome a hurdle that was preventing you from reaching your goal.

Step 36: Time and Money Saved
Talk to them about how you spent money and time trying to overcome a particular hurdle until you finally created the tool. Explain that this won't happen to them because you will provide the tool for them.

Step 37: Eliminate Doubts about Your Tools
Talk about false beliefs the audience may have regarding the tools or their complexity. Break those beliefs quickly and rebuild new ones.

Step 38: The Second Stack Slide
Show the same slide as before but now include the tools underneath the masterclass. The total price of the offer should also increase.

Step 39: Introduce First By-Product
This by-product is related to Secret 1, and is a physical product that participants will receive once they invest. Tell the audience the benefit of this by-product.

Step 40: What You Went Through

Talk about what you went through, emotionally and financially, before you finally created the first by-product. Explain why they don't have to endure the pain because you will be giving them the by-product as a bonus.

Step 41: Benefits of the By-Product

It doesn't matter the cost and pain you went through. Tell them why and how the bonus will make their journey faster and easier.

Step 42: Eliminate Related Beliefs

Whatever false beliefs they may have regarding the bonus and their ability to make use of it should be addressed now. As before, break and rebuild belief patterns.

Step 43: The Third Stack Slide

By now you should have figured out how a stack slide works. Below the first two elements, add the bonus to the stack. Don't worry about sounding repetitive. For you to sell effectively, the offer must be understood completely.

Step 44 - 53: Second and Third By-Products

Introduce the next two tangible products and go through steps 39 to 43. Explain the costs and pains involved in creating them, and reveal the benefits of the by-products. Eliminate all related beliefs, and then create a stack slide for the second (stack slide 4) as well as the third by-product (stack slide 5).

Step 54: The Full Stack
Your full stack should contain everything on offer and their prices. Sum up the grand total and make sure the value of the total is 10 times the real price.

Step 55: Use If/All Statements
Once you reveal the full value price, you have to get them to believe that your offer is worth it. Take each of your three secrets and create If/All statements for each one. For example:

For Secret 1:
If all this diet technique did for you was_____(linked to Secret 1), would it justify the price $_____?

You then wait until the audience responds in the affirmative. Repeat for Secrets 2 and 3 and then give them a discount. Since the total value of the offer was 10 times greater than the actual price, the audience will believe that they are getting a 90% discount.

Step 56: There Were Two Options
This can be an effective way of closing the deal because it leads the audience to agree that they are better off paying more to receive a better program.

> "There were to options available to me. I could make the program cheap and sell more products. But this would mean you wouldn't receive the real value. So I had to pick the other option, where though you invest more money, I get to dedicate more resources to ensure your success."

Step 57: What is It Worth to You?
You need to get the audience to ask themselves what achieving their goal would be worth to them. How much would they pay to get the product that will guarantee them success? Pause between questions to give them time to ruminate on the answer. Ask them to consider the money as an investment and not a cost.

Step 58: Drop the Price
Show them the slide containing the total value of the package on offer. Tell them what the total price is and how it compares to what everybody else pays. Then tell them that you are about to make them a special offer.

Step 59: Reveal the Price

Reveal to them the discounted price that is available to participants who respond to your call-to-action. Tell them to call in, visit a website, or click a link. Make sure that every slide that follows this one contains a link for signing up.

Step 60: Justify the Price

Though most people would end their sales presentation by showing a slide containing the price, you need to take some time to justify why you are charging so much. As the audience is still considering whether to buy or not, show them just how much they would pay if they weren't part of your presentation. Compare your price with what you are charging on your regular website or what other experts are charging.

Step 61: You Have Two Options

Mention the two options they have.

"You have two options right now. You could sit there and not take action, and not benefit from the information you have learned today. Or you could step out in faith and test the product to see what happens.

Step 62: Guarantee
Mention that they won't lose anything if the product doesn't bring them success because you have a 30-day guarantee as part of the offer. If they test it and it doesn't help them, they get their money back.

Step 63: No-Brainer Decision
Help them see just how simple this decision is.

"Think about this for a second: Is spending a couple of minutes checking this out worth it to you? Even if the product only achieves 50% of what I claimed it would, it will still be worth the money if _____."

Step 64: Last Stack
Now you show them the slide that contains the entire offer and its total value. Go through every item to get them to focus on the offer one last time.

Step 65: Create Urgency and Scarcity
This is where you market your product by throwing in a bonus that is only available for a limited period. Mention that the special offer will only be for the first X number of people or for a limited period of time. You could also offer both options.

This part is critical so don't avoid it if you want people to grab your offer immediately. Most people who leave never return to buy later on. In fact, you should offer a bonus to only those who are watching the live presentation rather than replays. Maintaining a deadline is critical.

Step 66: End the Presentation
In this final slide that ends the presentation, show the following components:

- Highlights of what is on offer
- Prices
- Countdown timer set for 30 minutes
- Call to action

Keep this slide up during your Q&A session with the audience. Go through your pre-written or live questions, and repeat the call-to-action after you answer every question.

And that, ladies and gentlemen, is what we call the stack. This one concept has the potential of generating more profits for you than any other technique. Learn and become a master at it. This is the ultimate gift that you can take away from this book!

CLOSING THE PRESENTATION

There are two potential ways of closing your presentation. You can do a "trial close" or use a close all through your stack. Let's take a look at each one of these options and how to use them effectively.

Trial Close
This is a simple technique that you can use to get your audience to buy whatever you want them to. A trial close is where you ask the audience multiple yes-or-no questions throughout your presentation. Of course the only credible answer is yes, so before long, you will have the majority of people in the audience nodding their heads as you speak. The questions you ask should be relatively simple and subtle so that the audience responds only in a subconscious manner. By the time you ask them to buy your product, they won't have any other option but to say what they've been saying all along – Yes.

If you have a webinar, find a couple of places that you can subtly insert trial closes. For example:

- Can we get started?
- Does this make sense?
- That's exciting, right?

If you can get the audience to say yes repeatedly, they will find it easier to accept your epiphanies as well the offer you are making them.

The 16 Best Closes For Your Stack
The list below is quite comprehensive, so pick the closes that will be most effective for your presentation and your offer.

1. **Money is Just a Tool**

You need to get your audience to see money as merely a means to an end. They should not fear spending money if they are doing so in exchange for something much greater. Convince them that money has no value on its own until they use it to buy something of value.

2. **Disposable Income**

Show your audience that after receiving their paycheck and paying the bills every month, most people spend their disposable income on flimsy expenses that are not fulfilling or don't lead to their growth. But they now have the opportunity to channel that monthly disposable income into a program or product that will help them achieve one of their goals.

3. **Money Comes Back**

Though there will always be disposable income at the end of every month, time lost cannot be replenished.

Show them that they can save time by working with you instead of wasting time researching how to achieve their goals by themselves.

4. Change Your Life
This close is all about convincing them of why it's important to invest today; otherwise, they will simply slip back to their old habits and never achieve anything.

5. Information Alone
Use this close to make them see that gaining information is great, but without someone to coach you and hold you accountable, success will be difficult to achieve. Explain how videos and PDFs provide information but having a guide to walk them through it will massively increase their chances of success.

6. Quit the Excuses
Tell your audience that it's time to choose between making money and making excuses. They cannot do both. They have to decide what kind of person they want to be.

7. Your Two Options
Explain to the audience why your prices are high so that they can agree with you. Tell them there were only two options: charge a low price, sell many

products, and not provide real value; or charge a higher price and provide everything they need to achieve success.

8. Their Two Options

Use this close to get them to see how crazy it is not to take advantage of the offer. They can either risk nothing and achieve nothing, or invest immediately and potentially reap a reward. If it doesn't work for them, they'll still get their money back.

9. Doers vs. Dabblers

Use this close to get people to identify themselves as either a doer or a dabbler. They can have faith, take action, and achieve something; or they can sit, not do anything, and get stuck in life.

10. Holding Hands

Close by offering to walk them, step-by-step, through the process of signing up. Explain clearly where they have to click and how to fill in any forms.

11. Say Goodbye

Use this close to show them how their lives will change for the better if they invest. They will say goodbye to all the stress and worry of not having enough money, time, energy, etc.

12. Compare Lives

Close by comparing the kind of life they have now and the life they will lead after investing in the opportunity.

13. Call Out Excuses

You need to mention those excuses that may be holding some people back and then eliminate them. Some may be worried about the setup being too technical or hard, while others may think it costs too much. Explain why each excuse is not valid.

14. Reluctant hero

Use this close to show them that you don't have to be special in any way to succeed using the system/new opportunity.

15. What They Already Got

This close is used to reveal to the audience just how much they have already benefited from the presentation even before they have spent a dime. Go ahead to tell them the extra benefits that accrue when they choose to invest in your offer.

16. Final Close

Use this close to push the undecided ones over the fence. Repeat to them clearly what steps to take if they want to sign up. Mention the name of the signup link or website and remind them of the money-back guarantee.

These are the 16 closes that will help you sell to your audience. Now that you are an expert at delivering the perfect presentation, let's turn our attention to the various funnels that you can use week in and week out.

PART IV: THE FUNNELS

It wouldn't hurt for us to spend some time reviewing your journey so far, would it? Your mass movement is now taking shape. You have identified your charismatic character, discovered a cause worth following, and created a new opportunity. You are now an expert at convincing people by delivering your message through storytelling. You have learned how to craft killer sales presentations using stories that stir desire in your audience; they can't help but want to buy from you. And now you know how to make people take action by creating a stack.

So what's left? The people to sell to, of course! This is where a sales funnel is required.

In Part IV of this book, we look specifically at ClickFunnels, a software that allows you to constantly bring people to you so that you can share with them the new opportunity and get them to become your followers.

THE PERFECT MODEL FOR YOUR WEBINAR AND FUNNEL

Most people who are in the information business have a specific model that they follow. In this model, you create an offer, sell to the audience, and then create a different product to offer to the same people as before. The problem with this model is that you have to come up with a new product every month, and soon enough, you will hit a glass ceiling in terms of profits.

The perfect model, however, is quite the opposite. How, you say? You use the same webinar week in and week out for 12 months straight! Here is a summary of what to do:

- Your schedule for your live webinar will span an entire week. So if you decide to hold your webinars on Thursdays, start promoting it on Monday until the day of the event. Send emails, use Facebook ads, and work with partners to get people to sign up.
- Once the webinar begins, stop promoting the event.
- Present the webinar and make your special offer.
- Show replays from Friday to Sunday midnight.

- At midnight, stop the offer and convert prospects into buyers.
- Start promoting the SAME webinar from Monday, but this time; you will add extra details and explanations based on questions that the audience asked.

And that's it! Keep refining and adjusting the same webinar, and promote it to different categories of audiences every week. Don't give up even if things get rough in the beginning. You will soon start to hit consistent numbers.

7 Steps to the Perfect Webinar Funnel

1. Direct Traffic to Your Webinar Signup Page
In the final chapter of this book, we shall discuss how to bring people to your webinar. Right now we are focusing on creating the perfect registration page. The biggest factor that determines your traffic is curiosity. To increase curiosity about your webinar, use an image that is a bit strange but related to your topic. You should also choose a headline that makes people want to find out more about what you are offering.

2. Direct Registrants to Your Thank-You page
This page contains basic information about the webinar, including a video of you talking passionately

about what you are offering them. Use this page to sell the registrants something even before they attend the live event. Alternatively, offer them a free trial of your product.

3. Send Introductory Videos

There's a lot that could happen between signing up and the live event that could distract registrants and prevent them from attending. For this reason, you can send them videos to keep the webinar fresh on their minds. The videos can pre-sell your new opportunity and maintain their excitement.

4. Send Email Reminders

If the webinar is on Thursday, send an email reminder 24 hours in advance; the morning of the event; 1 hour before; 15 minutes prior to; and just when the event begins.

5. Present a Live Webinar

The event should be 1 ½ hours long, with the first hour dedicated to breaking and recreating false beliefs. Spend the final 30 minutes making your pitch. After that, take 15 to 30 minutes answering audience questions and closing people. Usually, around 25% of the people who registered attend the event. If your attendance rate is lower than 25%, put more energy into sending regular email reminders.

6. The Follow Up

After the webinar, send emails containing a link of the webinar replay. You can also send PDF cheat sheets for those who love reading text over watching video. The goal with follow-ups is to create urgency to buy before the cart closes.

7. Cart Closed

If your webinar was on Thursday, make sure that at midnight on Sunday, you close the cart by deactivating the Buy button.

8. Repeat

On Monday morning, it's time to go back to step 1. Keep refining your presentation skills, Q&A session, and ad targeting. Don't give up even if nobody attends your event. Keep doing it on a weekly basis for 12 months, and before you know it, you will become a wealthy expert.

CLOSING IN FOUR QUESTIONS

In this chapter, we shall be dealing with how to close expensive offers that are in the range of $2,229 - $100,000. Unlike lower offers that involve sending the audience to a page with an order form, high-level offers require the additional step of phoning the prospect to create rapport and also determine whether they fit into your program.

The Four-Phase Script
There is a specific phone script that you can use to close high-level clients. This script may contain four major questions, but there are many follow-up questions that you can add to clarify the client's answer.

Phase One
Before you get on the phone, the prospect must fill a prequalification application form. Then contact the prospect and set up the call. The call should begin in a direct manner with minimal chitchat. Introduce yourself and explain to them that you will be asking them four questions, and how they answer will determine whether to keep going or not. If the prospect agrees, ask them the first question:

1. Imagine if we started working together now and I helped you learn everything possible to achieve your goals. Now imagine yourself 1 year from today. What personal and professional changes would lead you to believe that our partnership was the greatest decision you have ever made?

The goal here is to hear their inner desires, so if they can't answer this question, drop them. Most prospects will begin by talking about external desires like increase in monthly income or a new house. Ask follow-up questions to determine why they want to achieve these desires. This will prompt them to reveal their inner desires, and this is your cue to move forward.

2. You know what your desires are, so what's preventing you from achieving them?

The goal is to discover any obstacles blocking their path so that you can see if you are able to help. If they begin to blame others or external circumstances for their problems, they won't make a good client. Listen to those who take responsibility of their lack of knowledge of how to make their dreams work. Then ask them:

3. Are there any resources or talents you possess that you aren't maximizing on that I can use to help you overcome obstacles and reach your goals?

Get the prospect to think about possibilities and keep asking them to mention more ideas. Then review everything you have discussed so far. For example:

"It seems you know what your desires are, and you said you want _____ because_____. Your biggest obstacles have been _____ and _____, correct? And it appears you have resources that you are not really leveraging, correct?"

At this point, talk about how you handled such obstacles in the past. Ask them how their lives would improve if you helped them overcome the obstacles and maximize their resources. The prospect should be excited about the possibility, so ask the last question.

4. Are you interested in my help?

Don't say a thing until they respond. When they say yes, explain to them how the process works. Tell them your fee and what they get out of the opportunity. Finally, ask their permission to be transferred to your assistant who will handle their financial details. If they say they can't afford it, offer them a payment package.

This is how you close a prospect in just four questions!

PERFECT WEBINAR CHEAT SHEET

Is it possible for you to create the perfect webinar in a matter of minutes? This may sound impossible, but the truth is that with 15 minutes and a whiteboard, it can definitely be done!

In this chapter, we are going to run through the key guidelines that you can use to create a webinar when you are under pressure to present a live webinar in only 15 minutes. All you have to do is ask yourself and answer a few familiar questions.

Question One: What new opportunity am I offering?
Explain to the audience what new opportunity you can give them on top of what you normally do.

Question Two: What One Thing can I make the audience believe about my offer?
Use something similar to the big headline that you created earlier in the book. Give the presentation a title like "How to Lose 30 Pounds in the Next 30 Days Using This Technique."

Question Three: What can I offer to those people who decide to buy?
Find something special from your stack that you can give your buyers as part of a special offer.

Question Four: What story can I tell as my epiphany story?
Pick a story from one of your many epiphany bridge stories.

Question Five: Which 3 false beliefs does the audience have regarding the new opportunity and which epiphany stories can I tell them to eliminate those beliefs?
Use the false beliefs we talked about earlier: beliefs about the vehicle; beliefs about their ability to take action; and beliefs about external forces. Then think of three epiphany stories that will break each false belief.

Then what?

Now that you've cobbled together your content, you will have to promote your message to as many people as possible with very little time left. At this point, you can use your Smartphone to record your presentation and broadcast via Periscope and Facebook Live. This will work great if you already have a large following on these social media platforms. Just talk to the audience following the five questions you just prepared and close your sales.

These guidelines are guaranteed to work if you find yourself with very little time to come up with a live webinar event.

EMAIL SEQUENCE FUNNEL

It is possible to use the Perfect Webinar system in diverse areas of your marketing strategy, not just when creating webinars. One area that it can be of great benefit is in your email marketing. Every time you add a new customer onto your email list, you send them an email containing an epiphany story that is designed to hook them to the next email. Think of it like a soap opera series where you watch one episode and can't wait for the next one just to find out how the story ends.

Think of it this way; if you can use the format of the Perfect webinar for your Facebook Live webcasts as well as in a video sales letter, why not also incorporate it into your email funnel? You can even decide to use emails to make all your sales instead of inviting your audience to attend presentations.

All you have to do to make this work is break down your epiphany stories and insert them into every email you send out to your audience. You can choose to write the epiphany stories or alternatively, you can make a video for each story and insert a link to the video in every email. It doesn't really matter what format the story is received. The important thing is the structure you use to tell the story.

Just make sure that the emails are linked together to form a sequence of stories that intrigue and inspire your audience. Treat each email as a teaser so that your audience will be waiting on tenterhooks for the next one!

PART V: WHAT NOW?

Your presentation is ready and your funnels are good to go. But how do you ignite the masses and get them to follow you? Here's how...

FILLING YOUR FUNNEL

Everyone wants to know how to create traffic. That is always the big question. However, you don't have to create something that is already there. All you need to do is find a way to draw people from where they are online into your funnel.

Your Dream 100
If you dig deep into whatever industry you are in, you will discover that there are 100 people who have the customers that you desire. What you need to do is find a way of attracting these dream customers to come check out your opportunity instead.

Remember the three markets we identified earlier (wealth, health, and relationships)? If you step back into the submarket level, you will discover that all the traffic you dream of is right there. Now you have to find WHO is controlling it all.

Traffic is generally controlled by four categories of people/companies:

- Bloggers
- Influencers on social media
- List owners
- Podcasters

Identify and write down a list of 100 of these people and organizations (25 per category). Now you need to establish relationships with everyone on your list. It is always best to build relationships early so that by the time you want them to help you with something, the relationship will already be strong.

Here are three strategies for building your Dream 100 relationships:

- **Strategy 1** – Follow them, send them friend requests, subscribe to their lists, buy their products, and listen to their podcasts. You need to acquaint yourself with these people so that you know them well before making that crucial first contact. Be prepared by arming yourself with information.

- **Strategy 2** – Once you have them all figured out, offer them the opportunity to appear on your blog or podcast for an interview. This will promote them as well as help you build a stronger relationship from that 30-to-60-minute interview.

- **Strategy 3** – Once you have established a relationship with them, ask them about an important project that they are currently involved in. When they give you an answer, try to find a way to add value to their project to help them attain their goal. And voila! You have built a solid business relationship!

There is no better time to start using these strategies than NOW, even if you are still a small company. The next logical step is accessing their followers. If you are in the same niche, you will be competitors, but if you created your own niche, you can work together to promote one another. Here are three promotion strategies you can use:

- **Promotion Strategy 1** – Keep working the relationship until you are able to get your new opportunity in front of their followers. You can simply make a request for them to promote your webinar. You can also send them monthly newsletters and packages containing information regarding special promotions and ways they can partner with you. Some people will refuse, but be persistent. All you need is one Yes to hit it big.

- **Promotion Strategy 2** – It's OK if your Dream 100 cannot promote your product directly. You can still use social media to gain access to their followers. Use Facebook and Twitter advertising platforms to promote to followers of particular influential people and organizations. Create ads specifically targeting the followers of everyone in your Dream 100. Just make sure that you keep updated with changes in your social network of choice.

- **Promotion Strategy 3** - The final strategy can be SEO, marketing, and what is known as "integration marketing." This is simply offering your products within the sales flow of the Dream 100. Your offer should be integrated seamlessly into their sales funnel. For example, you could get one of your products to be promoted in their Thank-You pages. You can place your ad at the end of one of their emails. You can even collaborate on creating and promoting a product to boost both of your traffic flows. You can be as creative as you want when you are planning on using integration marketing.

There are numerous ways of filling your funnels, but this Dream 100 strategy is the best by far. As long as you have understood how it works, you can use whatever tactics you need to get new people to flow into your funnels.

CONCLUSION

Whoa! What a ride that has been! You probably feel overwhelmed by now with all the content that you have had to engorge on. However, all this is actually a shortcut.
So where do you even go from here?

Here are four things to take away from this book:

1. Know clearly who your audience is and the new opportunity you are offering them.
2. Test your idea using a beta group so that you are sure of having a solid foundation to build your business.
3. Learn how to weave great stories.
4. Go out there and change lives of people using your message.

This book has shown you how you can start with an idea and end up with a mass movement. You may think that your business idea is too small or not worthy, but I am here to tell you that you can use the system explained in this book to do wonders with that idea. There are many others who have done it and gone on to become multi-millionaires – and so can you.

I also hope that you have learned that a business is more than just personal growth and making money. You must also focus on contributing to society and helping others achieve their dreams. That is what you should take away from this book. A fulfilled life is one where you improve your own life and impact the lives of others.

Please take the time to learn all the skills described here and start putting them into action. With dedication, determination, and discipline, you will soon be able to move your business and customers to a greater level.

RESOURCES

Blue Ocean Strategy by W. Chan Kim and Renée Mauborgne

Dotcom Secrets by Russell Brunson

The One Sentence Persuasion Course by Blair Warren

The True Believer, Eric Hoffer

The Hero's 2 Journeys by Michael Hauge and Christopher Vogler

The Question by Dan Sullivan

If My Product's So Great, How Come I Can't Sell It? By Kim Klaver

www.FillYourFunnel.com

www.FunnelHackAThon.com

www.ProjectClickFunnels.com

www.2CommaClub.com

THANKS FOR READING

We hope you enjoyed this book. If you found this material helpful, please share it with a friend you know would love it too.

You can also help others find it by leaving a review where you purchased the book. Your feedback will help us continue to write books you love. Your one simple act of sharing could change someone else's life. Just so you know, the Entrepedia library is growing by the day so be sure to check out some of the other awesome books we offer. We recommended a few for you to start with on the last page of this book.

Also, we would love to hear your thoughts personally. Email us at feedback@entrepedia.co and let us know how we can improve our books.

Tell us, what it would take for us to create something you would want to tell everyone you know about?

Thanks

Remember
Receive 5 FREE Entrepreneur books by visiting
www.Entrepedia.co/FREEbooks

Get Your Entrepreneur Quick Start Guide here
www.Entrepedia.co/QuickStart

OUR MISSION

Entrepreneur Encyclopedia aims to accelerate the availability of useful information and aims to publish a high quality insightful book on every major topic in entrepreneurship.

Entrepedia hopes to remove barriers in sharing by taking the copyright off everything we publish and donating it to the public domain. We believe Copyright is hinders the sharing of information and ideas and instead only promotes a scarcity mindset. We hope other publishers and authors will follow our example. In addition, it is our goal to donate $1,000,000 or more by 2020 to help people in emerging nations access the capital they need to build fresh water systems, create a startup economy and enhance their local communities through entrepreneurship.

Doesn't it feel good knowing that as you educate yourself you are helping the world become a better place? We think so too.

Cheers to an epic future!

Travis and the Entrepedia Team

WHY ENTREPRENEUR ENCYCLOPEDIA WAS STARTED

Every time I wanted to capture a complete grasp of something new I'd have to buy 20 books on the topic and spend way too long sorting through them and everything online until I arrived at the big picture or receive any actionable insight.

I wished someone else would go in and figure out which information would impact me most and present it to me so I could quickly and easily devour it then apply it to my business. I couldn't find anyone doing this with quality in the entrepreneur space and figured I would just have to do it myself.

I wanted Entrepreneur Encyclopedia to curate the most helpful content in the field and put the best of the best information in little packets on every subject imaginable. I also wanted the topics to be readable within half an hour. That way I would be able to make time to read one or more books a day and fill my idea jar with knowledge.

By creating and sharing these books, Entrepreneur Encyclopedia aims to save you time and money. My team and I do all the research up front so you don't have to. Our goals is to sort through the best content on each topic, extracting the most complete understanding possible in under 30 minutes.

The quicker we can learn a wide variety of topics the sooner that information can begin playing a role in shaping our results now. And all the better if we can also make a positive difference in the world while doing it. That's why I focus on entrepreneurship and giving back. I know how hard it is starting from scratch so I'm donating 5% of this company's profits to fund micro loans from people with a vision but don't qualify for traditional funding.

We're also planting a tree for every 10 hard covers we sell and challenging ideas about copyright's place in today's world. As a company we have to be doing everything we can to support the ecosystem we all live in. I hope you join me in making this possible by supporting Entrepreneur Encyclopedia.

Thanks for reading,

Travis

If you enjoyed this book, you might also like Smart Reads

Smart reads delivers the same **compact information books** on a wide variety of topics outside of entrepreneurship. Here are a couple books you might find helpful:

The 30-Day Focus Plan: Achieve Laser Focus and Cut Through Noise in this Distracting World

Twitter Marketing Strategies: Smart Tips on How to Monetize Your Followers

How to Master Email Marketing: Your 1-Page Marketing Plan to Grow a Massive Email List, Make Money and Build Your Brand with Email

Writing on the Internet: Learn SEO Tips & Techniques and Become a Successful Online Writer

Change Your Mind Change Your Life: Control Your Life By Changing The Way You Think

Overcoming Procrastination: Proven Strategies on How To Improve Focus, Get Things Done and Achieve Your Goals

www.ingramcontent.com/pod-product-compliance
Lightning Source LLC
Chambersburg PA
CBHW050104230526
45470CB00004B/1670